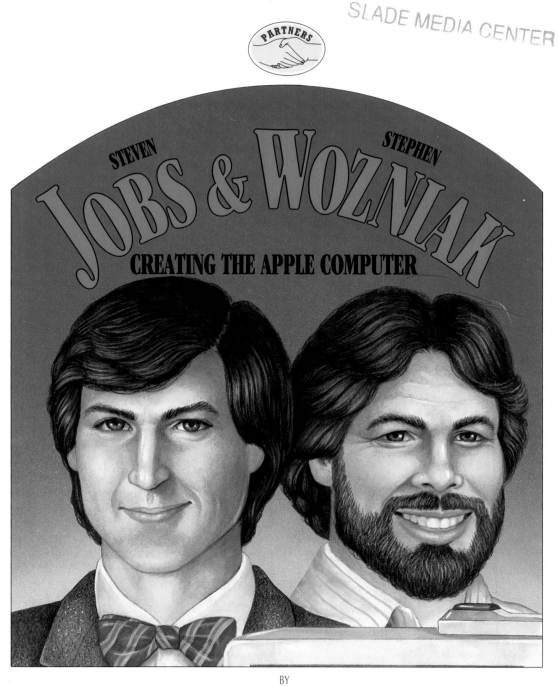

PARTNERS

STEVEN
STEPHEN
JOBS & WOZNIAK
CREATING THE APPLE COMPUTER

BY
Keith Elliot Greenberg

Illustrations by James Spence

A BLACKBIRCH PRESS BOOK

WOODBRIDGE, CONNECTICUT

Published by Blackbirch Press, Inc.
One Bradley Road
Woodbridge , CT 06525

©1994 Blackbirch Press, Inc.
First Edition

Printed in Hong Kong

10 9 8 7 6 5 4 3 2 1

Library of Congress Cataloging-in-Publication Data

Greenberg, Keith Elliot.
    Steven Jobs & Stephen Wozniak: creating the Apple computer / by Keith Elliot Greenberg. —1st ed.
        p.   cm.
    Includes bibliographical references and index.
    ISBN 1-56711-086-X   ISBN 1-56711-120-3 (Pbk.)
    1. Jobs, Steven, 1955– —Juvenile literature. 2. Wozniak, Stephen Gary, 1950– —Juvenile literature. 3. Computer engineers—United States—Biography—History—Juvenile literature. 4. Apple Computer, Inc.—History—Juvenile literature. [1. Jobs, Steven, 1955– . 2. Wozniak, Stephen Gary, 1950– . 3. Computer engineers. 4. Apple Computer, Inc.] I. Title. II. Title: Steven Jobs and Stephen Wozniak.
QA76.2.G73   1994
338.7'6100416'0922—dc20
[B]   94-20400
                                                CIP
                                                AC

⚜ Contents ⚜

Chapter 1. **Learning to Love Computers**   5

Chapter 2. **Whiz Kids**   8

Chapter 3. **Changing the World**   21

Chapter 4. **Chip in the Empire**   31

Chapter 5. **Moving On**   38

Glossary   47

Further Reading   47

Index   48

From the time they were kids growing up in California, Steven Jobs and Stephen Wozniak loved to invent.

Learning to Love Computers

It was not so long ago that many Americans were uninterested in using computers. Most computers were large and heavy. And most people believed that these complicated machines were mainly created for scientists and professors, not just ordinary folks.

Today, computers are everywhere. Children sit at the family computer to do homework and play games. Executives carry small computers in their briefcases. Schools all over the United States have computer rooms, where students go to do research and learn the most up-to-date programs.

How did such a change come about? The computer revolution is due, in large part, to two friends from California who shared an interest in invention.

5

Steven Jobs and Stephen Wozniak were both kids who had trouble fitting in with other kids their age. Instead, they amused themselves by coming up with inventions. In the early 1970s, Steven and Stephen were meeting with other local "computer fanatics" and playing with new technology. Less than a decade later, the two men had developed the revolutionary Apple II—a computer that anyone could use.

Each partner played a special role. Stephen Wozniak—known to friends as "Woz"—was the designer. Steven Jobs was the salesman. Woz connected the wires and circuits. Steven tried to get the public excited over their product.

According to Woz, Steven had never even "gone through a computer manual. But it never crossed my mind to sell computers. It was Steve who said, 'Let's...sell a few.'"

The Apple II was different from other computers because it was "user friendly." That meant a person with no computer knowledge could easily figure out how to operate the machine.

Once it was ready to sell, Steven and Woz attracted people to their Apple II through various techniques. The computer's colors were cheerful and inviting. The body was light and easily portable—an improvement over the bulky machines that came before. Most of all, the Apple's instructions were clear and easy to follow.

Perhaps the greatest reason for the Apple II's success was the partners' love of computers. To them, developing their product was first and most importantly an enjoyable hobby—not a method of making money. Because they had fun creating the machine, it was easy to convince their users that computers were fun, too.

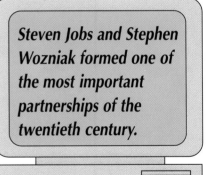

Steven Jobs and Stephen Wozniak formed one of the most important partnerships of the twentieth century.

Part of the fun was the fact that customers could see the personalities of Steven and Woz in every Apple computer. Amusing little drawings were designed to represent different functions on the screen. Eventually, funny sounds and graphics made the programs even more entertaining. As a result of their approach, Steven and Woz became millionaires at a very young age. More importantly, they will forever be remembered for forming one of the most important and influential partnerships of the twentieth century.

Whiz Kids

Steven Jobs and Stephen Wozniak were children of California's Silicon Valley. Located about 35 miles north of San Francisco, this region began to draw engineers, technicians, and inventors in the 1950s. It seemed that everyone in the region was puttering with some type of invention. By the time they were in elementary school, Steven and Woz considered experimentation and invention to be as much a part of growing up as playing baseball or watching television.

Steven the Curious

Steven Paul Jobs was adopted by Paul and Clara Jobs soon after his birth in 1955. Paul Jobs tended to change occupations often, working as a machinist, debt collector, and mechanic. The family also changed homes a great deal. By the time Steven was five years old, he had lived in three California towns: Palo Alto, San Francisco, and Mountain View, a town in the Silicon Valley.

From the day he started school, Steven was exceptionally curious. He often asked his teachers question after question—so much so that some of his teachers complained he was a "pest."

He also had a stubborn streak that angered his teachers, family, and friends. Although he loved learning—and spent much of his free time playing with chemistry sets and other educational toys— Steven hated being told what to do. At age nine, he announced that he refused to do his school work. Unable to change his behavior, his mother finally had to offer her son a prize just to go to class!

Yet, when Steven wanted to participate in a school project, no one showed more enthusiasm. At Cupertino Junior High School, he entered the science fair and displayed a device that controlled alternating electric current. He'd first gotten interested in the subject while sifting through garbage. In front of an engineer's house, he found a microphone

Steven first became interested in electronics when he found some electrical equipment in a neighbor's garbage pile.

connected to a battery and speaker. Unable to figure out what triggered the object's pulsing sounds, Steven went to his father for advice. When Paul couldn't answer his son's inquiries, Steven knocked on the engineer's door. The man admired the boy's thirst for knowledge so much that he offered to provide the youngster with lessons on electronics.

Unfortunately, Steven didn't get along with his peers as well. He was considered odd, and he was frequently targeted for practical jokes and other mean pranks. In junior high school, the situation had gotten so bad that Steven told his parents he wanted to drop out.

As it turned out, the Jobs family decided to move to another town, Los Altos, California. It was there that Steven enrolled in Homestead High School, and met Stephen Wozniak. Unlike others in the area, Woz was proud to call Steven his friend.

Stephen the Loner Genius

Woz was five years older than Steven, and equally influenced by the technology in the Silicon Valley. Woz's father was an engineer for Lockheed in Cupertino. His specialty was designing satellites.

For Woz, inventing was a great way to ease the loneliness and frustration of being an "outsider."

Like Steven, Woz grew up feeling that he was a loner. But Woz discovered early on that inventing and investigating the uses of electricity helped to ease his loneliness. Eventually, Woz found a group of friends with the same interests and, together, they often performed numerous experiments.

By the time Steven was in high school, he was visiting with Woz and his friends, discussing— among other issues—computers. With Woz's encouragement, Steven also joined the electronics club at Homestead High School.

Hard Work Pays Off

Whenever the electronics club needed supplies, Steven worked on the problem until he found a solution. He once called a parts manufacturer collect, explaining to his teacher, "I don't have the money for the phone call. They've got plenty of money." Another time, he phoned Bill Hewlett, a founder of the Hewlett-Packard company—and ended up not only with electronics parts, but with a summer job as well!

Steven spent his time at Hewlett-Packard building computers on the assembly line. He dreamed of one day building a computer of his own, but he realized that he didn't have enough technical knowledge. To reach his goal, he needed friends with a better understanding of these complicated machines—friends like Stephen Wozniak.

Phone Stunts

Steven had always thought of himself as a person who lived by his own rules, doing things when and if he felt like it. In Woz, however, Steven found not only a friend, but a role model. The younger boy looked up to Woz, and listened closely to his ideas.

"I was nowhere near as good an engineer as Woz," Steven later told *Time* magazine in an interview. "He was always the better designer."

Having always felt like a bit of an outlaw himself, Steven couldn't help admiring a particular war Woz was waging against the telephone company. It had all started when Woz read an article in his mother's *Esquire* magazine about special "blue boxes" that enabled people to illegally make free telephone calls. The boxes imitated and repeated the same tones that were used by the telephone company to provide service and connect lines.

Steven and Woz sometimes misused their knowledge of electronics by interfering with the local phone company's service.

Soon, Woz was part of an international network of "phone phreaks"—known by names like "Cap'n Crunch" and "Dr. No." These people transmitted information to each other by computer and illegally made free calls all over the world.

"I would get on the phone all night long and try to figure out how I could work my way through...the worldwide phone system," Woz recalls.

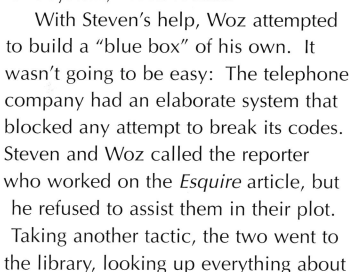

The boys were talented, but they were often mischievous. Wrongly, they even broke the law once or twice.

With Steven's help, Woz attempted to build a "blue box" of his own. It wasn't going to be easy: The telephone company had an elaborate system that blocked any attempt to break its codes. Steven and Woz called the reporter who worked on the *Esquire* article, but he refused to assist them in their plot. Taking another tactic, the two went to the library, looking up everything about the technology.

Still, they couldn't figure out exactly how to get their blue box to work. Once, they tried to call Woz's grandmother in Los Angeles. After many mistakes, they managed to phone the city, but they reached the wrong number.

Steven and Woz refused to give up. They contacted the most famous "phone phreak" ever, Cap'n Crunch—who got his name by using the whistle in cereal boxes to imitate telephone tones. He met with them, and provided important tips. He also cautioned them to always use a pay phone, to prevent the telephone company from tracing the call.

Soon, the partners had a blue box that worked. Although they knew that they were breaking the law, they didn't seem to care. Learning the technology and breaking codes was far too much fun to worry about the law.

College Troubles

With their passion for investigating, experimenting, and inventing, Steven and Woz seemed like the types of students who would thrive at college. But this wasn't true. Both Woz and Steven had trouble at school, and both ended up dropping out.

Woz had enrolled as an engineering major at the University of California at Berkeley in 1971, but he never graduated. While others his age were hard at work in class, Woz was going to meetings of the Homebrew Computer Club. This was a group he formed with others who were interested in computers and new technology concepts. After dropping out of school, Woz was so poor that he often had to borrow computer chips from friends to complete his experiments.

Steven and Woz were so fascinated by electronics that little else, including school, could hold their attention.

After finishing Homestead High in 1972, Steven registered for classes at Reed College in Portland, Oregon. Reed was known for its students who "questioned authority." Not only did Steven rarely show up to his classes, he gave up his dorm room and lived with different friends on the campus. Finally, he dropped out, rented a room in Portland, and told his family he planned to teach himself.

Not surprisingly, Steven's parents were furious. They refused to send their son any more money. After working at an animal laboratory at the college repairing electrical equipment, Steven moved back home in 1973. In California, he found a job designing video games for Atari. Video games were a brand new pastime, and Steven was both fascinated and inspired by the technology that made them possible.

Taking a Chance

Woz had also landed an interesting job—with Hewlett-Packard. While there, he had also built his own computer, and continued to attend meetings of the Homebrew Computer Club.

"I wasn't too interested in making money," Woz recalls. "I just liked Homebrew. It was the most important part of my life."

After a long trip to India—where he studied the philosophy of the country's gurus, or spiritual teachers—Steven returned to California. Those who saw him upon his return could not believe their eyes. Steven had shaved his head and was wearing traditional Indian clothes! But it was not long before he got back into his old, familiar routine. And when he first saw Woz's computer—a television screen that was connected to a keyboard—Steven had a vision. He would bring this machine to the world.

After many years of wandering around aimlessly, Steven felt he finally had a direction. He decided to start a company with Woz. Woz would design the computers, and Steven would sell them. Soon, they decided, the creations would be used by people everywhere.

Soon after he returned from his trip to India, Steven began to attend meetings of the Homebrew Computer Club.

Convincing Woz was the tough part. After all, he had a wife, a child, and more responsibilities than his independent friend. But Steven was so sure of success that he convinced Woz to take a risk. Woz quit Hewlett-Packard, and entered into a partnership that would soon make him more rich and more famous than he had ever dreamed possible.

• 3 •

Changing the World

Before the duo could begin selling computers, their company needed a name. One day, Steven remembered the joy he once felt while picking apples in Oregon. That was it. Steven suggested naming the company Apple. He said that anyone who could come up with a better suggestion had until 5 P.M. to do so. But nobody did. So, on April Fool's Day, 1976, the Apple Computer company was officially born.

While Woz designed the new computers, Steven worked on the logo—or company's symbol. He finally settled on a drawing of a small apple with a bite taken out of it.

21

With limited funds, the two partners opened their first office in Woz's apartment. Papers and spare parts were everywhere, and Woz's wife and child barely had any space for themselves. After a while, Apple Computer had to shift operations to a spare bedroom at Steven's parents' home. When that got too crowded, Steven's father took his car out of the garage and the company moved there.

At this point the two young businessmen needed extra money, but no one would give them a loan. The partners were young, and neither had ever had much success at anything. Finally, the two decided that they had to sell whatever they owned to keep going. Steven got rid of his prized Volkswagen microbus, and Woz sold his good calculator. Now, they had $1,300—not much, but enough to stay in business.

The partners' first computer, the Apple I, was designed for people who considered computers a hobby, but couldn't build one. Steven remembers, "The customers for the Apple I were Woz and me and our friends in the Homebrew Computer Club."

But Steven and Woz knew that their business couldn't survive with only their buddies as clients. The two hired a number of people to come up with

When they first started their company, Steven and Woz had their office in Woz's apartment.

ways to reach a wider audience. Their investment paid off when the Byte Store, a new computer shop, ordered 500 machines. Word began to spread through California that two Silicon Valley computer fanatics were on the verge of something big.

Introducing the Apple II

In 1977, Steven and Woz unveiled the Apple II. After observing the problems people had experienced with the Apple I, the partners believed they had now created a much improved machine.

"A lot of people who wanted to use the product were unable to," Steven said of the Apple I. To change this situation, the pair put the computer in a case and added a keyboard. Now, the product was no longer just for computer fans. Now, almost anyone could use it.

The young inventors were also willing to learn from the mistakes they had made before. "If there hadn't been an Apple I, there would not have been an Apple II," Steven recalls. "The first product solved some of our problems and exposed the remaining ones in a much clearer light."

In addition, Woz and Steven always tried to put themselves in the place of the people who'd use their computers. "Woz and I cared from the very beginning," Steven says. "And we felt that the people who were going to own the Apple II would care, too. We were selling these things for $1,600, I think, which was a lot of money back in 1977,

and these were people who generally didn't have
$1,600. I know people who spent their life savings
on one." Because of this loyal following, the partners always cared as much about what the Apple II
looked like on the outside as how it was
put together on the inside.

The new machine attracted not only
individuals, but businesses interested in
modernizing their procedures and trans-
ferring their files onto computer. About
16,000 programs would soon be written
for the Apple II—catering to everyone
from secretaries to executives to children who were just interested in playing
computer games.

Steven and Woz learned from their mistakes and constantly tried to improve their product.

As interest grew, Woz and Steven invested both
their skills and their emotions in the product. Steven
would get so excited at meetings that he'd occasion-
ally start crying and have to take a walk outside to
calm down.

Soon, the best in the business world heard about
the success of the Apple company. A.C. ("Mike")
Markkula—a salesman for the computer chip company, Intel, and a millionaire at age 30—invested

In 1977, Steven and Woz introduced the Apple II, which was designed to be especially easy to use.

$250,000 and became Apple's chairman of the board. Pepsi Cola's John Sculley was then hired as the company's president. His task would be running the business end of Apple on a day-to-day basis.

In the meantime, Steven concerned himself with building and expanding the company's ideas. He also became very involved in quality control.

Steven said that he and Woz wanted to create "an environment in which excellence is noticed and respected...If you have that, you don't have to tell people to do excellent work. They understand it from their surroundings. You may have to coach them at first, but then you just get out of their way, and they'll surprise you time and time again."

Expanding Fast

By 1979, the days of operating out of Steven's parents' garage was over. Apple was now in a small building in Cupertino, close to where Woz grew up and the junior high school where Steven starred in the science fair. The employees—many of whom already loved computers as a hobby—realized the impact that Apple was having on the lives of ordinary Americans. Because of that, Apple's workers put great passion into their jobs. People came to work early and left late. Woz and Steven rewarded workers with bonuses and stock, which were percentages of the company. When customers walked in off the street to buy computers, employees would applaud and congratulate each other.

In late 1980, Apple began selling stock to all who were interested in owning shares. Investors rushed to buy up the offerings. By the end of the first day, Apple's worth had boomed to $178 billion. "Everyone wants a bite of Apple," the financial newspaper, *The Wall Street Journal*, declared.

Jobs and Woz now had more money than they could ever hope to spend. But their main interest was still creating the world's best computers. For four years, the company worked on the Lisa, introducing it in January, 1983. Some considered the Lisa to be an improvement over the Apple II, but the price tag was quite high—about $10,000. Later in the year, the company started selling a more affordable version of the Lisa, called the Macintosh. The staff—now numbering 70—had reason to be proud of the innovation. Employees had spent 90-hour, seven-day-weeks making sure the Macintosh was close to perfect.

Despite the prosperous turn of events, the computer company—now divided into divisions for Apple and Macintosh—refused to lower its high standards. Steven would show up at the Macintosh factory and would inform its manager, Debbie Coleman, that he was going to inspect the building's cleanliness. "I'd put on a white glove to check for dust," he remembers.

When Debbie Coleman got annoyed at Steven's strict standards, Steven explained his belief about taking pride in even the smallest part of your job. "It wasn't going to be the big things that would stop us," he said. "It was going to be the little details [that would keep] these machines running."

Steven was so concerned about quality control at the Apple factory that he personally inspected it for dust on a regular basis.

·4·

Chip in the Empire

Companies built on dreams sometimes experience difficulty when they grow too big, too soon. Often, a casual, friendly atmosphere can be replaced by a formal office in which many workers do not know each other's names. When this happens, the founders have to answer to investors, salespeople, and a doubting press. The energy that originally drove the partners can then be replaced by wondering if the enterprise is really worth all the headaches.

Like so many other businesses, Apple Computer Company endured serious growing pains in the early 1980s. And slowly, old friends Woz and Steven found themselves drifting in separate directions.

Near Tragedy

In early 1981, the Jobs and Wozniak partnership almost ended tragically when Woz was involved in a serious airplane crash.

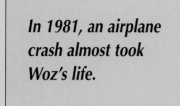

In 1981, an airplane crash almost took Woz's life.

Wealth had enabled Woz to pursue expensive hobbies, including flying. On one particular day, he was piloting a Beechcraft Bonanza airplane. During take-off at a small California airport, he suddenly crashed, and injured his head badly.

Fortunately, he survived his injuries. But Woz was left with amnesia—an inability to recall certain things. One year after the episode, he still could not remember the wreck.

The incident forced Woz to take a leave of absence from Apple. But as his memory slowly returned, he grew sentimental, longing for the days he spent experimenting with computers in Steven's garage. After two years, he returned to the company, promising to boost morale there.

"I've got enough money to sit back in the pool and watch it all go by," he said. "But I want to be in life."

Concert Promoting

Before joining Apple again, Woz wanted to live out another dream. One day while driving in his car, he listened to a string of hits by his favorite groups. Why, he wondered, don't great bands play on stage back-to-back like on radio? As a millionaire, Woz was in a position to do something about this. In 1982, he promoted the Us Festival—featuring groups like The Police, Fleetwood Mac, and The Grateful Dead—over a three-day period near San Bernadino, California.

About 200,000 people attended the musical event, listening to tunes blasting from a 400,000-watt sound system—the best of its kind at the time. Woz spent $12.5 million of his own money to make sure everything went as he imagined.

The Us Festival wasn't supposed to be an average rock concert. Woz said the theme of the event was to "unite us in song." Through music—and computers—he aimed to teach young people to care for one another. Instead of asking, "What's in it for me?" he promoted, "What's in it for us?"

Grateful Dead lead singer, Jerry Garcia, said the festival helped to spread the word that computers

In 1982, Woz spent $12.5 million of his own money to produce the Us Festival in California.

were for everybody. "Technology used to be scary," he said. "Computers used to be seen as cold, emotionless. Now, people are realizing there's flesh and blood in computers, and excitement and thrills, and room for all things that are human."

Throughout the concert, Woz walked through the crowd, asking spectators, "Are you having a good time?" People would rush up to him and kiss him. The statement heard most often—and the one he claimed to find most satisfying—was, "Thanks, Woz."

Friends Drift Apart

Plenty of Apple employees would have expressed similar feelings of gratitude. By 1983, about 300 workers—many who had been awarded generous shares of stock—were millionaires.

Still, nothing seemed to be able to repair the wounds already opened at the company. The Macintosh was not selling as well as Steven had hoped. As the company continued to spend money to improve the Macintosh division, those working for Apple were angry. At times, it seemed like the company was split into two hostile camps: the Macintosh camp and the Apple camp.

John Sculley—the man Steven had hired to over-see business affairs—decided to take an extreme measure. He fired 1,200 people at Macintosh. Then, at a meeting on April 22, 1985, he delivered gloomy news to Steven. The co-founder of Apple was being removed as the head of Macintosh.

After Steven took a leave of absence from the company, he met with Sculley to mend the relation-ship. Steven agreed to remain on Apple's board of directors. And Apple said it would fund ten percent of a new company Steven wanted to start.

But the peace was shortlived. Steven recruited Apple employees for his new operation. The Apple board of directors believed he was stealing their most talented workers, and refused to supply him with any more money. Additionally, they accused him of robbing Apple of its high-tech secrets. Soon, they fired him.

This was not the type of climate Woz wanted to be a part of. Apple was no longer a friendly place to work, and in 1985, Woz officially retired from the company.

From that point on, Apple had to continue with-out the two men who first gave it life.

❧ 5 ❧

Moving On

Their departure from Apple by no means signalled the end of the two men's involvement in the world of technology. Both Woz and Steven continued doing what they always had—experimenting and trying to introduce the world to new concepts.

Fulfilling Other Dreams

In 1986, Woz finally achieved a goal he had long desired. Fifteen years after first enrolling at the University of California at Berkeley, the 35-year-old graduated. He had returned to the college in 1981, and had quietly attended classes, for the most part unrecognized. Few other students noticed him

In 1986, Woz graduated from the University of California at Berkeley, achieving a lifelong goal.

because he registered under a fake name: Rocky Raccoon Clark (after the Beatles song "Rocky Raccoon").

The same year, he teamed up with Atari founder Nolan Bushnell—builder of the first video game ever—to create a game called TechnoForce. Woz loved video games, and had ten in his home. "The thrill I get playing with my kid is equal to the thrill I got designing computers," he explains.

TechnoForce took video games a step further. This was a battle between small robots that fired infrared beams at each other and were powered by remote control. Bushnell described the invention as "a video game coming to life."

In 1987, Woz devised another gadget: a remote control that could turn on a video recorder, change a television channel, lower the volume of a stereo, and operate certain appliances with one command.

Developing such contraptions reminded Woz of the days he and other wild whiz kids tinkered with their crude computers and telephones. Longing to keep his roots in focus, Woz co-founded the Electronic Frontier Foundation in 1990. This was an organization that provided legal assistance to "hackers"—people who tested their technical knowledge by breaking into hidden computer networks. Some criticized this move, since hackers sometimes break the law. But this was how Woz got started, and he wanted to give something back.

Steven Heads into the Future

Steven left Apple to create a company called NeXT, which developed a computer with 5,000 times more power than the Macintosh. The machine's icons—symbols for programs and functions—were cartoons rather than dull emblems. Students could use the computer to study a variety of subjects on the same screen. At a conference in San Francisco, Steven played a violin duet—with the computer.

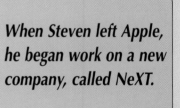
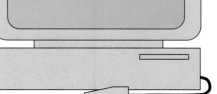

When Steven left Apple, he began work on a new company, called NeXT.

"We're going to change the way teachers teach and students learn," Steven said to his audience.

Steven claimed he wanted to hear everyone's ideas at the company, and didn't mind being challenged. "People feel fine about openly disagreeing with me," he said. "That doesn't mean that I can't disagree with them, but it does mean that the best

The NeXT computer was 5,000 times more powerful than the Macintosh, but it did not do well with the public.

ideas win. Our attitude is that we want the best. Don't get hung up on who owns the idea. Pick the best one, and let's go."

Steven realized that it would be difficult to outdo his already legendary reputation. Recalling that he and Woz "were in the right place at the right time" to influence the computer industry, Steven adds, "I hope the NeXT machine will contribute as well."

Unfortunately, Steven's newest creation did not cause the sensation he had anticipated. Most users complained that the computer was slow and too expensive. Sales did not reach the forecasted numbers. Some reporters wondered if the computer industry's golden boy was "losing his touch."

Steven, however, viewed his problems with his usual confidence. "Oh, we'll make a whole bunch of mistakes," he said. "That's what life is about. But at least they'll be new and creative ones."

A Life at Home

Having changed the technical and business worlds with their revolutionary ideas, Steven and Woz devoted themselves to bettering their personal lives in the early 1990s.

In 1992, Steven and his new wife Laurence, had a baby boy and settled down to family life.

On March 18, 1991, Steven married Laurence Powell, a Stamford University business student—after giving her an engagement ring worth over $500,000. The next year, the couple had a son.

Parenthood, says Steven, "changes your world. It's almost like a switch gets flipped inside you, and you can feel a whole new range of feelings that you never thought you'd have."

Woz was also dealing with family responsibilities, marrying for the third time in 1991. With six children, he decided to expand his house in the Silicon Valley town of Los Gatos.

Neighbors complained that Woz's new home was more like an amusement park than a residence. Indeed, there was a limestone cave, with replicas of crystal formations, dinosaur footprints, fossils, prehistoric drawings, and rock carvings. "The whole house has to be for kids as well as adults," Woz said. "Kids just love secret places."

Despite their wealth, success, and fame, Stephen Wozniak and Steven Jobs will forever be kids at heart themselves—two very creative kids from the Silicon Valley who taught the world to love computers and the magic they can create.

The partnership between Steven and Woz will always be remembered as one that changed the face of daily life in the world.

Glossary

blue box Box used to copy telephone tones in order to get illegal, free phone calls.

byte Smallest amount of information a computer can handle.

hacker Person who breaks into hidden computer networks.

icon Symbol for computer program or function.

logo Company symbol.

stock Percentage of ownership in a company.

user friendly Easy-to-use computer.

Further Reading

Hill, John. *Exploring Information Technology.* Austin TX: Raintree Steck-Vaughn, 1992.

Murphy, Linda. *Computer Entrepreneurs: People Who Built Successful Businesses Around Computers.* San Diego: Computer Pub. Ent., 1990.

Rozakis, Laurie. *Steven Jobs: Computer Genius.* Vero Beach, FL: Rourke, 1993.

Wicks, Keith. *Working With Computers.* New York: Facts On File, 1992.

Index

Apple Computer Company, 28–31
 Apple II, 29, 36
 early days, 20–25
 Lisa, 29
 Macintosh, 29, 36, 37, 41, 42
 naming, 21
 stock offering, 28
Apple I, 22, 24
Apple II, 6–7, 24, 25, 26
 See also Apple Computer
 Company.
Atari, 18, 40
 TechnoForce, 40

Bushnell, Nolan, 40
Byte Store, 23

Coleman, Debbie, 29
Cupertino, California, 11, 28

Electronic Frontier Foundation, 40

Garcia, Jerry, 33

Hewlett, Bill, 13
Hewlett-Packard, 13, 19, 20
Homebrew Computer Club, 17, 19,
 20, 22

Intel, 25
Jobs, Clara (mother), 8
Jobs, Paul (father), 8, 11

Jobs, Steven
 birth, 8
 childhood, 8
 at Cupertino Junior High School,
 9, 11
 at Homestead High School, 11,18
 marriage, 45
 meeting Stephen Wozniak, 11
 at Reed College, 18
 trip to India, 19

Lockheed, 11

Markkula, A.C., 25

NeXT Computer Company, 41, 42,
 43

Powell, Laurence, 44, 45

Sculley, John, 26, 37
Silicon Valley, California, 9, 11, 23, 45

Wozniak, Stephen
 airplane crash, 32
 childhood, 13
 computer club. *See* Homebrew
 Computer Club.
 at Homestead High School, 11, 13
 at University of California at
 Berkeley, 17, 38
 Us Festival, 33, 34, 36